SRI RAMANA MAHARSHI

SRI RAMANA MAHARSHI

Sage of the People

Anupa Lal

Revised Edition

RUPA

Published by
Rupa Publications India Pvt. Ltd 2015
7/16, Ansari Road, Daryaganj
New Delhi 110002

Sales centres:
Bengaluru Chennai
Hyderabad Jaipur Kathmandu
Kolkata Mumbai Prayagraj

Edition copyright © Rupa Publications India Pvt. Ltd. 2002, 2015

Text copyright © Anupa Lal 2002, 2015

All rights reserved.
No part of this publication may be reproduced, transmitted,
or stored in a retrieval system, in any form or by any means,
electronic, mechanical, photocopying, recording or otherwise,
without the prior permission of the publisher.

The views and opinions expressed in this book are the
author's own and the facts are as reported by him which
have been verified to the extent possible, and the publishers
are not in any way liable for the same.

ISBN: 978-81-291-3674-9

Third impression 2025

10 9 8 7 6 5 4 3

The moral right of the author has been asserted.

Typeset by Ninestars Information Technologies Ltd, Chennai

Printed in India

This book is sold subject to the condition that it shall not,
by way of trade or otherwise, be lent, resold, hired out, or otherwise
circulated, without the publisher's prior consent, in any form of
binding or cover other than that in which it is published.

CONTENTS

Sri Ramana Maharshi	7
Chapter One	11
Chapter Two	16
Chapter Three	22
Chapter Four	28
Chapter Five	34
Chapter Six	40
Chapter Seven	48
Chapter Eight	56
Chapter Nine	62
Bibliography	68

SRI RAMANA MAHARSHI

All eyes in the large crowd were on the open doorway of the small room. He lay inside, his body weakened and shrunken after many months of painful illness. Soon after sunset he asked his attendants to sit him up. A doctor tried to give him oxygen but he waved him away. Suddenly devotees outside his room began singing Arunachala Shiva, a beloved hymn he had himself composed with much emotion. For a moment his eyes opened and shone, tears of bliss trickling from them.

He took one more deep breath—and then no more. At that very moment, an enormous star trailed slowly across the sky towards the peak of Arunachala, the sacred hill.

8 • SRI RAMANA MAHARSHI

'When beggars die there are no comets seen
The heavens themselves blaze forth the death of princes.'

And yet this 'prince' among men lived a life more austere perhaps than a beggar's. Always barefoot, clad only in a loin-cloth, his worldly possessions—a walking stick and a water pot. He lived practically without food for months at a time, begged for food in the streets when necessary, consistently refused special treatment in the *ashram* that grew up around him and to which rich and poor thronged alike.

This extraordinary personality was the gentle sage of Arunachala, known to the world as Bhagavan Sri Ramana Maharshi.

CHAPTER ONE

Sri Ramana Maharshi was born into a middle class Brahmin family on 30th December 1879, while the festival of Arudra Darshan (the sight of Lord Shiva) was being celebrated. He was the second of three sons and a daughter, born to Sundaram Aiyer, a pleader in the town of Tiruchuzhi in Tamil Nadu, and his wife Alagammal.

When Venkataraman (as he had been named) was twelve, his father died and the two elder boys moved to the house of their paternal uncle in Madurai, where Venkataraman attended the American Mission High School. He was a boisterous, athletic boy, more interested in swimming, wrestling and football than in his studies. He did, however, have an amazingly retentive memory.

One of the pranks he played as a child was to get into the locked house of a neighbour, a lawyer, remove some important papers and distribute them to people in the street as if they were advertisements for a forthcoming play!

When the prank was discovered, Venkataraman's father was furious. 'Undress the boy,' he ordered, 'Give him only a loin-cloth to wear. Shave his head completely and let him stay without food!'

Years later, after he had attained enlightenment and reached the Arunachala Temple, Venkataraman re-enacted this punishment. He had his head completely shaved, threw away all his clothes except for a loincloth and stayed practically without food for several months.

From childhood, the word 'Arunachala' as something grand and sacred, had always fascinated Venkataraman. In 1895 he met an elderly relative coming from there and was thrilled to discover that Arunachala actually existed on earth and could be visited.

The second premonition of the path, towards which his destiny was taking him, came soon after when he read the *Periapuranam*, the life stories of sixty three Tamil saints and was overwhelmed with joy and wonder. A few months later came the sudden awakening that changed his life forever.

He was sitting alone in a room in his uncle's house in Madurai when a violent fear of death took hold of him. Holding his breath and lying like a corpse, he mentally began to examine the reality of death. 'My body was silent and inert but I felt the full force of my personality and even the voice of the 'I' within me, apart from it. I was the Spirit transcending the body. Fear of death had vanished once and for all. Absorption in the Self continued unbroken from that time on. Other thoughts might come and go like the various notes of music but the 'I' continued like the fundamental *sruti* note that underlies and blends with all the other notes.'

In such simple and direct words did Ramana Maharshi later describe the overwhelming experience of Self Realization or merging with God, which according to Hindu belief is the goal of human existence, but which takes many lifetimes to achieve.

Obviously such a momentous occurence in the life of a mere schoolboy, with no special spiritual training, brought changes that his family and friends were bound to notice. He lost all likes and dislikes with regard to food. He became submissive where he had earlier been assertive with other boys, not complaining or retaliating no matter what happened. He stopped going out to play games with his friends, preferring to stay by himself, and became even more disinterested in his studies. Almost every evening he went to the Meenakshi temple which had not attracted him earlier and stood before the images of the gods and saints, overcome by emotion.

Seeing him sitting alone in meditation, Venkataraman's elder brother Nagaswami would jeer at him, calling him a *yogi* and tell him to retire to the forest as so many ancient *rishis* had done. Nagaswami and his uncle felt that Venkataraman was neglecting his duties which were to get an education so that he could begin to earn for the family.

Matters came to a head on the morning of 29 August 1896, about two months after the experience of Self Realization. Seated in the same room, this time with his elder brother, he found he could not continue doing the homework assigned to him. He pushed it aside and sitting cross-legged, began to meditate. Annoyed, his elder brother said sarcastically, 'What use is all this to such a one?' He meant that his brother had no right to want to live life a *sadhu* or renunciative and enjoy the comforts of home life at the same time.

Venkataraman realized that his brother was right. There and then he decided to renounce everything and set out in search of Arunachala, for him the holy of holies. He hid his intention from his brother and uncle, who he knew would have stopped him, but wrote a farewell note to allay their anxiety. Taking just enough money—three rupees—which he thought would cover the journey, he left home.

CHAPTER TWO

It took him three days to reach the town of Tiruvannamalai, close to the holy hill of Arunachala. He travelled most of the way by train and also walked for several hours when his money ran out.

On his second night away from home, he reached the temple of Arayaninallur. He entered the pillared hall and sat down. Suddenly a brilliant light illuminated the dark temple, for which he could find no explanation. After some moments the vision faded and he sat down again in meditation.

On the morning of 1 September, Venkataraman arrived at the Tiruvannamalai railway station. From there he walked with eager steps to the temple of Arunachaleshwar, the great Lord Shiva. The gates of the high walls surrounding the temple were open. So were all the doors, including the one to the innermost shrine. Strangely enough, no one else was present as he entered and stood before the deity. 'Father I have come,' he said and his journey ended in the blissful peace of that union.

On emerging from the temple, Venkataraman had his head completely shaved and threw away the sacred thread he wore as a sign of his caste. Clad only in a loincloth, he took up his abode in the thousand pillared hall within the temple complex. Here he sat day and night, for weeks, hardly moving, never speaking, completely absorbed in his inner life.

The hall was open on all sides and so the still figure of the young renunciate aroused public curiosity. School boys often pelted him with stones to see, as one of them said later, if he were real or not. To avoid such harassment the Brahmana Swami (as he was known by then) shifted into the *Patala Lingam*, an underground chamber, below the thousand pillared hall, which was deserted but also permanently dark and dank. Here ants, mosquitoes and other vermins attacked him, leaving lifelong marks on his legs. But he continued to sit in meditation, unperturbed.

After a few weeks some *sadhus* bodily removed him from that unhealthy pit. He remained unconscious of his surroundings as they set him down before a temple dedicated to Subramaniya (the son of Lord Shiva). There he stayed for about two months, as still as a statue, deep in contemplation. A *mouni swami*, also observing silence, looked after him, bringing him a cupful of a mixture of water, milk, sugar, turmeric and fruit with which an idol in the temple was daily washed. It was his only nourishment until the temple priest substituted it with pure milk.

People had begun to notice and revere the silent young swami. But their swelling numbers were a source of disturbance for him. Despite his moving twice or thrice and then to the Gurumurtam temple outside the town, the number of visitors continued to increase. At the Gurumurtam temple, a Malayali *sadhu* named Palaniswami attached himself to the young sage and continued to serve him for the next twenty one years. There was little that he could do for his young master. Although food offerings poured in from devotees, all that the Brahmana Swami would accept was a single cup of food at noon. The rest was returned as *prasad*.

At Gurumurtam, a devotee discovered by chance that Venkataraman was literate. Another devotee persisted in his enquiries until he learnt the name and birthplace of the young swami. Information of his whereabouts eventually reached Venkataraman's family.

After about a year at Gurumurtam, he moved to a nearby orchard which could be locked to ensure privacy.

It was here that one of his uncles tried to prevail upon him to continue his austerities closer to home, so that his family could attend to his needs. But Venkataraman made no response and after five days his uncle returned to Madurai, disappointed.

A few weeks later, his mother and his elder brother found him in the temple of Pavazhakkunru, one of the eastern spurs of the Arunachala hill, to which he had shifted. Alagammal immediately recognized her long-lost son despite his wasted, uncared for body and matted hair. For days together she begged him to return with her, tempted him with tasty food, shed tears of reproach, but to no avail. Forced by others to respond to her in writing, if not in speech, he wrote, 'Whatever is destined not to happen, will not happen, try as you may. Whatever is destined to happen, will happen, do what you may to prevent it. The best course therefore, is to remain silent.'

Unable to get any other response from him, his mother and brother left for Madurai.

Not long after, in early 1899, the young sage moved to the Virupaksha cave on the south eastern slope of Arunachala. Here he stayed more or less for the next seventeen years. The cave named after Virupaksha Deva, a thirteenth century saint who had lived and been buried there, is shaped like the sacred syllable *Om*. It is said that the sound of *Om* can be heard within the cave.

In those days wild animals roamed freely on the hill. Venkataraman was once sitting with a devotee outside the Virupaksha cave when a leopard and a tiger started playing together in the valley below. Completely unafraid, he watched them with a smile until they left, refusing to retreat into the cave with his terrified devotee.

Even before he moved to the Virupaksha cave, he had begun to read books on spiritual knowledge. Characteristically, he did this not from a desire for learning, having already attained the highest knowledge, but to help a devotee. His Malayali attendant Palaniswami brought books from town to study, but since most of these were in Tamil, not Malayalam—his mother tongue, he struggled to understand them. The young master would go through the books and briefly explain the essence of their teaching to Palaniswami. The spiritual knowledge that the young sage already instinctively possessed, enabled him to grasp effortlessly whatever he read and retain it, because of his prodigious memory.

With the same ease he picked up Sanskrit, Telugu and Malayalam from books on spiritual philosophy as well as sciences with a spiritual base such as *ayurveda*.

Although devotees had begun to seek him out soon after he reached Tiruvannamalai, it was only now, after more than three years of silence, that he was prevailed upon to answer their questions. Initially he did this by writing his answers either on the ground, or on strips of paper, or with chalk on a slate. Among the devotees who preserved these answers were Gambhiram Seshayya and Sivaprakasam Pillai. His answers to their questions were later published as *Self-Enquiry* and *Who Am I*.

It was to Ganapathi Sastri, a well known Sanskrit scholar and a spiritual seeker for many years, that he gave his first oral instructions in 1907. It was Ganapathi Sastri who suggested that the old name of the young sage—Venkataraman—should be shortened to Ramana, adding the words *Bhagavan* (the Divine), *Sri* (blessed) and *Maharshi* (short for *Maha Rishi*, great sage). Most devotees came to address him simply as Bhagavan. Ganapathi Sastri's disciples now become devotees of Ramana. He answered their questions on the means to attain the highest truth. The most important of these questions and answers were recorded as *Sri Ramana Gita* and later published.

CHAPTER THREE

Arunachala, were Sri Ramana was to spend more than fifty years, is one of the oldest and most sacred holy places in India. According to Puranic legends, Lord Shiva appeared as a blazing column of light to settle a dispute between Brahma and Vishnu on who was superior. When both gods realized their folly, they prayed to Shiva to manifest himself in a form less dazzling so that ordinary mortals too could worship him. For the good of the world, Shiva manifested himself as Arunachala, the sacred hill. The gods declared that whoever circumambulated the hill slowly and with reverence would be blessed by Lord Shiva and his wishes would be fulfilled by the grace of the Lord.

If Ramana had a guru, it was Arunachala teaching in silence. 'What is a Guru?' he said to a devotee. 'A guru is God or the Self. First a man prays to God to fulfil his desires. Then a time comes when he does not pray for the fulfillment of a desire but for God himself. So God appears to him in some form or other, human or non-human, to guide him as Guru in answer to his prayer.'

Ramana always encouraged *pradakshina* (circumambulating or walking round a holy place). 'It does not matter if one has faith in the *pradakshina* or not,' he often said. 'Just as fire will burn on touching it, whether they believe or not, the hill will do good to all those who go around it.' He himself used to go round the hill with his devotees regularly from 1900 to 1926 until the crowds around him became unmanageable. There was no portion of the hill he did not know.

Aksharamanamalai, a hundred and eight verses in praise of Arunachala, were composed by

Ramana at the specific request of his devotees, as were nearly all his compositions. He set out one day on *pradakshina*, taking pencil and paper with him. As he composed the verses, tears of ecstasy streamed from his eyes. All the pain of separation and the bliss of union felt by a spiritual aspirant are mirrored in these glowing verses. This heartfelt poem is also an acrostic, Its one hundred and eight verses begin with the successive letters of the Tamil alphabet. When some devotees asked Ramana to interpret some of the verses, he said, 'You think it out and I will too. I didn't think while I was composing it. I just wrote it as it came.'

For several years after he came to Tiruvannamalai, Ramana lived on *bhiksha*, which was food obtained by begging in the streets. He often told devotees that begging for alms was a good antidote for the ego.

When he was still maintaining silence he would go into the town, stop at the threshold of any house and clap his hands. If food was given to him, he would receive it in his cupped hands and eat it standing there. He would never enter a house even if he were invited in. Every day he begged in a different street and never went to the same house a second time.

While he was staying in the Virupaksha cave the number of devotees staying with him gradually increased. Food was provided for their midday meal by other devotees. The evening meal was obtained by their going out to beg for food. Instead of asking for food at each house, the devotees would walk down the street singing *Akshara Malai*, a hymn composed by Adi Sankara. Householders hearing the hymn would recognize the singers as Sri Ramana's devotees and come out to offer them food.

Some local *sadhus* copied this routine. As a result they tricked the householders into giving them the food meant for Ramana's devotees! To rectify this situation, Palaniswami and the others asked Ramana to compose some verses they could sing to identify themselves when they went to collect *bhiksha*. It was in answer to this request that he composed the *Akshara-manamalai*, better known by its refrain—Arunachala Shiva.

Whatever the quantity of food brought to the Virupaksha cave, Ramana always shared it with all those present. Consequently very often there was not enough to go round.

'At times there used to be no *curry* or *chutney*,' Ramana reminisced. 'People were many while the food obtained was limited. What were we to do? I used to mix food into a paste and pour hot water over it to make it like gruel and then give a glassful to each and take one myself. Sometimes we felt it would be better if we had at least some salt to mix with it. But where was the money to buy salt? We would have had to ask someone for it. If once we began to ask for salt we would feel like asking for *dal*, then for *payasam* and so on. So we swallowed the gruel as it was. As the food was *satvic*, without spices, not even salt, not only was it healthy for the body but there was great peace for the mind.'

There were also days when there was no food to eat, followed by days of abundance. In both situations Ramana remained tranquil. He encouraged devotees to develop the same attitude, saying, 'Whenever we do not get food we should celebrate that day as *Ekadasi* (the eleventh day of the waxing or waning moon and traditionally a day of fasting). When we get plenty of food we should celebrate that day as *Dwadasi* (the twelfth day when the fast is broken with a feast).

A woman named Echammal was one of the devotees who cooked and brought the midday meal to Virupaksha cave every day. Before she was twenty-five years old Echammal first lost her husband, then her only son and then her only daughter. Devastated by her grief she left her village and went to various holy places in search of solace. But her grief remained. Then she heard of the young swami who lived in the Virupaksha cave. She climbed the hill and stood in silence before him. No words were spoken in the one hour she was there but the compassion shining in his eyes healed her of her sorrow.

From that day onwards she visited Ramana every day, spending the rest of the thirty-eight years of her life in Tiruvannamalai. Daily she cooked a meal for him and his devotees and carried it up the hill herself or had it sent if she were unwell. She did this even after regular meals began to be cooked in the *ashram* that came up later. One day the cooks forgot to serve the food that Echammal had sent. Ramana usually signalled to the others to start eating but this time he sat silent, refusing to start his meal. Everyone was puzzled and concerned. It was only when the cooks remembered to serve the food sent by Echammal that Ramana signalled that the meal should commence.

CHAPTER FOUR

When his mother first visited him in 1898, Ramana made it quite clear that family ties no longer existed for him. Despite that 'rejection' she continued to visit him. On one of these visits in 1914 she fell seriously ill with symptoms of typhoid. Ramana nursed her back to health. In 1916 she came again, this time to stay. Since Ramana had left home she had endured many bereavements. Her eldest son had died; then her brother-in-law, leaving the joint family in straitened circumstances. In 1915, the wife of her youngest son passed away, leaving behind a little boy. Alagammal turned in her grief and old age to her second son Ramana, to whom she could see so many others turning for support.

Ramana did not oppose her staying with him as many thought he might. But bit by bit, through word and deed, he changed and moulded her. She received no special treatment from him and if she complained he said, 'All women are my mothers, not you alone.' Slowly the sense of superiority at being the Maharshi's mother disappeared and she began to cook and care for all the devotees like a mother.

Scarcity of water had always been a problem at the Virupaksha cave. Soon after his mother's arrival Ramana moved higher up the hill where there was a perennial source of water. The new, more spacious accommodation was named Skandashram after the devotee who constructed it.

Ramana weaned his mother away from much of her orthodoxy. If her *sari* touched a non-Brahmin he would say in mock consternation, 'Look! Purity is gone! Religion is gone!' Despite the food cooked being strictly vegetarian, Alagammal, like very orthodox Brahmins, considered some vegetables impure. Again her son mocked this attitude. 'Mind that onion,' he would say, 'It is a great obstacle to *moksha*' (liberation)!

In the last years of her life Alagammal's son became her Guru as he was Guru to so many. She had glimpses of his divinity. Once he disappeared as she sat before him and she saw instead a column of pure light. She burst into tears thinking he had discarded his human form till he reappeared as the son she knew.

Alagammal passed away in May 1922. Ramana was with her throughout the final hours, not attempting to prolong life but to still the mind so that death could be an absorption in the Self, freedom from the mortal destiny of rebirth. Her body was interred at the foot of Arunachal and a shrine constructed at the spot. Her youngest son Nagasundaram, who had taken *sanyas* and joined the devotees in Skandashram, began living near the shrine in a thatched hut. Ramana came there from Skandashram almost daily, a thirty minute walk down the hill. After about six months, one day he did not return to Skandashram but simply stayed near the shrine. Devotees followed him and the present Ramanashram gradually came up there.

From 1922 to 1928 the *ashram* consisted of just two huts. Ramana lived in one with the other inmates. The second hut was used as a kitchen cum dining room. Gradually as the number of inmates increased and donations came in, single storeyed buildings were erected—a hall forty feet by fifteen, where Ramana stayed and met visitors, a dining hall and store-room, an office and book shop, a post office, a dispensary, a large dormitory and a few small houses for male devotees. The *ashram* was run by a committee headed by Ramana's

brother since he himself would neither handle cash nor the management of the *ashram*.

In June 1924, three men tried to rob the *ashram* one night. Ramana remained unperturbed and courteous even as the robbers broke windows, threatened the inmates and hit them with sticks. 'Take what you want,' he said, 'but there is very little. We are poor *sadhus* living on charity.'

All that the thieves were able to take were a few thin strips of silver for adorning deities, a few mangoes, a little rice and about ten rupees, most of them belonging to a visitor. When Ramana advised his devotees to attend to their injuries, they were enraged to discover that he too had been hit by the robbers.

Ramana said with a laugh, 'I also have received some "*poosai*"!' (a Tamil word for both 'beating' and 'worship').

But he held back a devotee who had picked up an iron rod and was going after the thieves. 'They are misguided men,' Ramana said. 'But we should not give up our *dharma*. If your teeth suddenly bite your tongue, do you knock them out in consequence?' The thieves were later caught and imprisoned.

This was not the only occasion when Sri Ramana faced hostility and aggression. Each time he remained unconcerned. Once he was sitting under some tamarind trees outside the Gurumurtam temple when some thieves came to steal the ripe tamarind pods. Seeing the young swami seated in silence, one of the thieves said, 'Put some sap in his eyes. That might make him speak.' The acid in the sap could have blinded Ramana, apart from causing him great agony, but he continued to sit calmly and the thieves did him no harm.

On another occasion a group of drunken *sadhus* appeared at the Virupaksha cave and declared that they had been sent by the ancient sage Agastya to give Ramana *diksha*, initiation, after extracting from his body those salts that prevented him from attaining higher powers. Ramana sat serenely impervious to their threats but a devotee who was present, put the fear of God in the tricksters. He began lighting a fire and announced that the same sage Agastya had informed him in a vision of the *sadhus'* arrival. The sage had also told him that they possessed great powers and could be boiled in hot oil without sustaining injury. By lighting a fire to heat oil for their immersion, he was only following the sage' instructions. Hearing this the drunken *sadhus* took to their heels.

CHAPTER FIVE

For almost twenty years, until 1949, Sri Ramana sat, stretched and slept on a couch in a corner of what some called Liberty Hall since humans and animals alike had the liberty to approach him there at any hour of the day and even night. Like all great sages, Ramana felt a oneness with all creation. Any injury to a plant or tree pained him and he tried to prevent it. He once remarked, 'You may call a tree a standing man and a man a walking tree.'

Until the Ramanashram was constructed, he lived serene and unafraid on a hill where there was abundant wild life. He would not permit snakes to be killed where he resided. 'We have come to their home,' he said. 'And we have no right to trouble or disturb them. They do not molest us.'

Monkeys roamed freely all over the hillside. Ramana watched them closely with the keen observation that was natural to him. He learnt to understand their cries, their code of behaviour and system of government. He discovered that each tribe had its king and its recognized district. Ramana told visitors that monkeys recognized him as one of their community and accepted him as an arbiter in their disputes.

A young monkey who had been badly bitten and left helpless by the others, arrived limping at the Virupaksha cave. Ramana looked after him till he recovered. He would sit in Ramana's lap, be given his own leaf plate to eat from and was a meticulously clean eater. Contrary to their normal practice of boycotting a monkey cared for by humans, the tribe took him back and he later became their king.

In Liberty Hall squirrels ran all over Ramana and he had to be careful while leaning back so as not to crush them.

One day a squirrel being chased by a dog ran past him. He threw his walking stick between the two to distract the dog, slipped as a result and broke his collar bone. But the squirrel was saved.

Dogs were also lovingly cared for and fed before he was. Whether it was coffee, food or sweets, these 'children' were served first. The ancestress of most of the *ashram* dogs was Kamala who came to Skandashram as a puppy. She was extremely intelligent and perfectly capable of showing a visitor around the hill when Ramana instructed her to do so.

Another animal with whom the sage had a unique and close relationship was a cow named Lakshmi. She came to the *ashram* as a calf in 1926 and lived there for twenty two years. She would come up the steps straight to Ramana in Liberty Hall and he would always have a tidbit for her. For many months she came punctually at lunch time to accompany him to the dining hall! Once when there was little grass growing in the *ashram*, Ramana noticed that Lakshmi was not getting enough to eat. That day he refused his meal saying it should be given to her. The workers in the cowshed realized their mistake. Fodder was bought from the *bazaar*, enabling both Ramana and Lakshmi to resume their meals.

When Lakshmi was dying, Sri Ramana sat beside her and took her head on his lap. Her laboured breathing became steady, tears trickled from her eyes and his eyes also overflowed. Lakshmi died peacefully and was buried in the *ashram* compound with full funeral rites, besides the graves of a deer, a crow and a dog whom Ramana had also had buried there.

Liberty Hall was always kept clean and tidy. It was swept several times a day. The cloths that covered Sri Ramana's couch were absolutely clean and carefully folded. The loin cloth, his only garment, was gleaming white. The two clocks in the hall always showed the correct time.

During the last decade of his life the door of the hall was opened at 5 a.m. Devotees entered and sat in meditation while the Vedas were chanted. At 6 a.m. Sri Ramana went to the bathroom and at 7 a.m. breakfast was served in the dining hall. From 8 a.m. to 11 a.m. devotees sat before him again in the hall with a break of half an hour at 10 o'clock when Sri Bhagavan walked for a while on the hill. During the last two years or so, rheumatism so crippled his legs that he could only walk slowly across the *ashram* grounds. Sometimes all those present in the hall sat in deep and peaceful silence. At other times questions were asked and discussed or songs were sung that devotees had composed in praise of their Bhagavan.

When the mail was brought in, Sri Ramana looked at newspapers and read letters which were answered by the *ashram* office staff. These answers were shown to him for approval the same afternoon before being despatched. Lunch was 11 a.m. As he grew old and frail Sri Ramana agreed to rest for a while after lunch. He was available to devotees again between 3 p.m. and 5 p.m. At 5.30 the chanting of the Vedas began again. An hour later women left the *ashram*, followed at 7.30 by the men. Then the evening meal was served. After a short time for silent meditation in the hall, everyone retired by about 9 p.m.

In the twenties and thirties when Sri Ramana was in good health the daily routine was somewhat different. He would be in the *ashram* kitchen between 2.30 a.m. and 4 a.m. cutting vegetables, grinding ingredients and preparing dishes along with the kitchen staff. He was a strict disciplinarian and did not tolerate any sloppiness or waste. Vegetable parings were never thrown away but used as cattle feed. He expected everyone to be as thorough and painstaking as he was. The way he prepared a humble vegetable like spinach was a lesson in patience, economy and culinary art.

Spinach was cut into three portions—leaves, stems and roots. The leaves were used for making curry. The stems were tied together, added to the boiling *sambar* and later removed. The roots of the spinach were cleaned several times in water and then crushed three or four times on the grinding stone. The juice was extracted each time until only fibre was left. This juice was mixed with the *rasam*.

This regular method of cooking spinach obviously entailed a lot of work and often Sri Ramana did most of it himself. Once the kitchen staff decided to save themselves some labour. They smuggled the roots out of the kitchen and buried them in a spot that Sri

Ramana did not often visit. That day while out walking, he did! He investigated the freshly disturbed earth with his walking stick and some of the roots appeared. Sri Ramana sat down and dug up all the buried roots. He cleaned them thoroughly, patiently extracted their juice, added it himself to the *rasam* and then continued with his walk. All this he did with a smile and no trace of anger. But he taught the shamefaced kitchen staff a lesson in thrift they never forgot.

Sri Ramana's homely, often unorthodox ways sometimes puzzled strangers. A longtime devotee once convinced a friend to visit the *ashram* and get the sage's *darshan*. When the man returned he said, 'What a useless *swami* you sent me to! I thought he would be engaged in divine worship, but on an *ekadasi* day he was actually cutting onions!' For orthodox Brahmins this was a double offence. They normally fast on *ekadasi* and they do not eat onions at all.

CHAPTER SIX

Sri Ramana always refused preferential treatment. He would not allow an electric fan to be switched on just for him in the hall. When his health declined, many devotees implored him to take more nourishing food than that routinely cooked in the *ashram*. One devotee suggested that Sri Ramana should drink a glass of orange juice every day.

'How can we afford such luxuries?' he replied. 'For us there can only be a poor man's rations.' The devotee said that providing one glass of orange juice daily for Bhagavan would not cost very much.

'No, no !' said Sri Ramana. 'We would require about two hundred glasses of juice daily for all the inmates. Do you want me to gulp down the juice alone?' Similar suggestions, even from longstanding devotees, were all dismissed. What could not be equally shared was like poison for him.

While Sri Ramana set an example by submitting to all the rules and regulations that came into force as the *ashram* grew bigger, he would not submit to those he considered unjust. Seldom did he protest or reprimand but let his behaviour focus attention on the injustice.

When the *ashram* management was unable to provide coffee for all those eating in the dining hall, those seated at the far end, away from Sri Ramana, were served just water. His sharp eyes noticed this discrimination. He asked for water too from then on and refused to accept coffee.

On another occasion when his knees were already stiff with rheumatism, a European visitor unaccustomed to sitting cross legged sat before the sage with her legs stretched out. She was pulled up by an attendant who did not perhaps realize how hard it was to sit cross legged if one was not used to it. Feeling ashamed, the lady hastily drew in her legs. Sri Ramana immediately sat up and did the same despite the pain in his knees. When devotees protested he said, 'If it is the rule to sit cross-legged I must obey it like everyone else. If stretching out one's legs is disrespectful, then I am being disrespectful to all those here.'

Even after the attendant asked the European lady to sit as was most convenient for her, it took some persuasion to get Sri Ramana to relax as before.

As indifferent as he was to his own body, its pains, its comforts, so was he thoughtful and caring about all those who came into contact with him. An *ashram* attendant's finger was crushed while carrying stones to a building site. Till the finger healed, Sri Ramana himself took on the attendant's work of carrying stones.

A hardworking building supervisor was sometimes late for lunch. One day when he was particularly late, a kitchen worker rebuked him. 'You may be working hard. So are we. You should come on time.' Sri Ramana overheard and said sternly, 'The work he was supervising would not have been properly done in his absence. If you need rest you may take it. I will feed the supervisor.'

In Skandashram an elderly devotee named Sowbhagyatamma took a vow not to eat until she had her Bhagavan's *darshan* for which she toiled up the hill every morning. One day she did not come. The next morning Sri Ramana asked her why. She explained that she had the good fortune of his *darshan* from her own house from where she had seen him sitting on a stone slab, brushing his teeth.

From that day, even when the weather was bad, Sri Ramana always brushed his teeth siting on that stone

for the benefit of Sowbhagyatamma and other elderly devotees who wanted his *darshan* every day but were too infirm to climb the hill.

Each devotee felt he enjoyed his Bhagavan's special grace. Pundits seeking elucidation of ancient texts received Sri Ramana's full attention as did a child who not to be outdone, came to Bhagavan with his book of nursery rhymes. The book was tattered. Thrifty and meticulous as he always was, Sri Ramana took the book, got it mended and bound and gave it back the next day.

People came to Bhagavan for consolation, for spiritual enlightenment or even out of mere curiosity. Each one was helped in accordance with his understanding, his devotion. 'The grace of a guru is like an ocean,' Sri Ramana said. 'If one comes with a cup he will only get a cupful. It is no use complaining of the niggardliness of the ocean. The bigger the vessel, the more one is able to carry.'

The answers he gave to questions were always adapted to the questioner and always apt. A visitor showing off his knowledge, described different spiritual paths and concluded, 'Which of them is right? Which way should I go?'

Sri Ramana remained silent. When the visitor persisted he said simply, 'Go the way you came.'

The visitor complained to devotees that this answer was unhelpful. They pointed out its profounder implications. The only way is to return to one's source, to go back the way one came. At the same time it was just the reply he deserved.

There were devotees who prayed to Sri Ramana whenever misfortunes assailed them. Their prayers were answered. Illness passed away or problems were resolved often at the very time that the appeal was being made to him. But he never spoke about his supernatural powers and discouraged his devotees from doing so. He reminded them that powers were only a distraction on the path to Self Realization.

Many times his compassion worked not in removing problems, but in granting peace and fortitude inspite of them. A woman widowed, a father whose only son had died, turned to him in their grief. He said nothing but the love and understanding that shone from his luminous eyes, healed their suffering.

And yet behind the compassion was 'the silent urging to give up the desires and attachments that made misfortune possible; to turn from the even frustrated ego to the ever-blissful Self' within each human being.

This was Sri Ramana Maharshi's real teaching, based on the ancient doctrine of *Advaita*, but shaped by him to suit our troubled times.

CHAPTER SEVEN

According to the philosophy of *Advaita*, the Self or Spirit alone exists. It manifests as all the changing forms of the universe, without itself ceasing to be both formless and changeless. But the human mind does not recognize this one stupendous truth. Each individual imagines himself or herself to be a real and separate being, just as a person in a dream may imagine himself or herself to exist apart from the mind of the dreamer. All human miseries and uncertainties are a result of ignorance.

However a person's ego has an intuition of the Self, conceiving it as a Higher Being, infinitely good, infinitely wise, which it calls God. The goal of human existence is to realize that one is not, and has never been, separate from this Being or God. And for that realization to come, the ego, or a person's sense of on individual self has to vanish. Sri Ramana often called it, 'disrealizing unreality so that Reality could appear.'

But how was this to be done? Innumerable seekers like Paul Brunton, a British writer, asked Sri Ramana this question.

'You have to ask yourself the question—Who am I?' Sri Ramana answered Brunton, speaking through an interpreter. 'This investigation will lead in the end to the discovery of something within you which is behind the mind. Solve that great problem, of who you actually are, and you will solve all other problems thereby. Man's real nature is happiness. Happiness is inborn in the true Self. Man's search for happiness is an unconscious search for his true Self, which is imperishable. Therefore when a man finds it, he finds a happiness which does not end.'

When Brunton asked, 'What exactly is this Self of which you speak?' Sri Ramana replied, 'To understand, it is first necessary for a man to analyse himself. Because he has never faced his "I" in the true manner, he has too long identified himself with the body and the brain. Therefore I tell you to pursue this enquiry "Who am I"?...'

'The first and foremost of all thoughts, the primeval thought in the mind of every man is the thought "I".

It is only after the birth of this thought that any other thoughts can arise at all. It is only after the first personal pronoun "I" has arisen in the mind, that the second personal pronoun "You" can make an appearance. If you could mentally follow the "I" thread until it leads you back to the source you would discover that, just as it is the first thought to appear, so it is the last to disappear. This is a matter that can be experienced.'

'What is left?' Brunton asked. 'Will a man then become unconscious or will he become an idiot?'

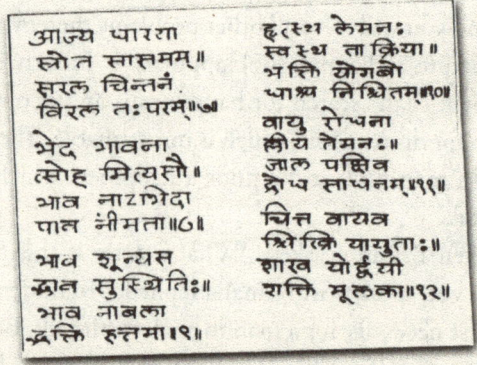

'On the contrary' answered Sri Ramana, 'he will attain consciousness which is immortal and he will become truly wise, when he has awakened to his true Self which is the real nature of man.'

'The sense of "I" pertains to the person, the body and brain, When a person knows his true Self for the first time, something else arises from the depths of his being and takes possession of him. That something is behind the mind; it is infinite, divine and eternal. Some people call it the Kingdom of Heaven, others call it the soul, still others name it *nirvana*. We Hindus call it *mukti* (liberation). When this happens, a man has not really lost himself, rather he has found himself.'

Sri Ramana explained that the attempt to turn the mind inwards through the method of Self Enquiry would gradually 'awaken a current of awareness, a feeling of the essential "I" who is the universal Self—unaffected by good or ill fortune, sickness or health. This awareness was to be gradually developed by constant effort until it became a constant undertone to all the actions of life.' Self Enquiry was not a meditation practice to be undertaken at certain hours, in certain positions. He often repeated that there was no need for a man to renounce the world in order to live a spiritual life. Giving up the ego, the false self, was the true renunciation. The ancient path of Self Enquiry had been followed for the most part, by sages living in silence and solitude, away from the hubbub of the world. Sri Ramana showed that the path could be followed by anyone, anywhere and right in the midst of worldly activity. There was no conflict he

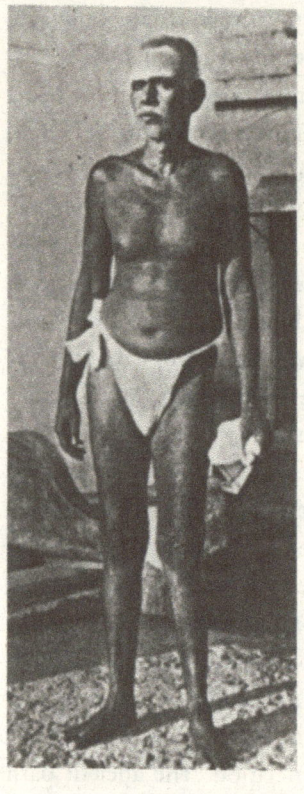

always said, between work and wisdom.

Self Enquiry, sincerely practised, even for a quarter of an hour a day, he told a devotee, would result after four or five months, 'in all sorts of unconscious clairvoyance, in peace of mind, in power to deal with troubles, yet always unconscious power.'

The path of Self Enquiry, like every spiritual path, requires pure, dispassionate living as well as intense spiritual effort. In moments of both pain and pleasure, the enquiry—who is hurt? who is pleased? who actually am I?—gradually destroys the I-am-the-doer, I-am-the-enjoyer or sufferer illusion created by the ego of the individual. Striking directly at the egoism in every action and reaction, the discipline of Self Enquiry, honestly pursued, does away with the need for any formal code of conduct.

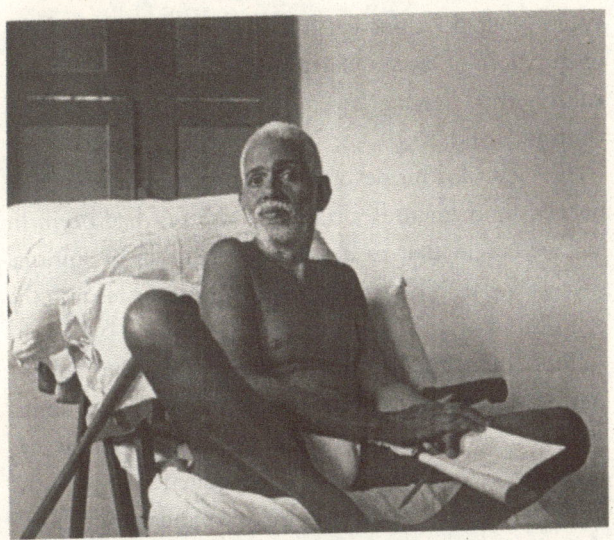

It makes it possible for a person to live serenely, without vanity, without attachment. Such an individual can attend to all aspects of her or his life because she or he remains unaffected by them, centred in the real Self within. Sri Ramana compared such an undividual to the cashier of a bank who handles lakhs of rupees calmly and efficiently because she or he knows the money does not belong to her or him.

However progress on the spiritual path is slow and requires constant effort. Sri Ramana warned devotees that 'the ego, oblivious of the Self, even when once made aware of it, does not get liberation on account of the obstruction of accumulated mental tendencies. Long cultivated tendencies are to be eradicated only by long continued effort.'

He never led his devotees to expect a miracle such as his own immediate Realization of the Self had been. In fact he taught that to desire or even think of spiritual success was in itself wrong because it meant feeding the ego instead of extinguishing it.

Sri Ramana referred to Self Enquiry as 'the one infallible means, the only direct one, to realize the unconditioned absolute Being that a human being really is. It was also the most accessible path since it required no rituals, no priests, no theory or philosophy to be understood.

But he also recognized how difficult a path it was to follow for many of those who came to him, and he never imposed it on any of his devotees.

He helped and guided them on whichever path they found most congenial to their emotional and spiritual needs.

The troubled souls who flocked to him for solace, felt his grace, his love, and surrendered their griefs and attachments to him. 'I don't understand the philosophy,' said a devotee. 'But when Bhagavan looks at me I feel just like a child in its mother's arms.' 'Those who were not at first drawn to seek the Self within, were drawn by love to the Self manifested as their Guru Sri Ramana. And he often said, 'Submission to God, Guru and Self is the same.'

The path of *Bhakti*, Devotion or surrendering the ego to a Higher Power and the path of *Gnana*, Knowledge, were not two different paths. As Sri Ramana explained it, 'The eternal, unbroken, natural state of abiding in the Self is *Gnana* or Knowledge. To abide in the Self, you must love the Self. Since God is in fact the self, love of the Self is love of God, and that is *Bhakti*. *Gnana* and *Bhakti* are thus one and the same.'

CHAPTER EIGHT

Although Sri Ramana patiently answered the questions that were put to him, real teaching was through silence. Effortlessly he emitted a silent power which calmed and purified the minds of those who came to him, far more effectively than words.

'How does speech arise?' he asked a devotee who had enquired why Sri Ramana did not preach to the people at large. 'First there is abstract knowledge. Out of this arises the ego, which in turn gives rise to thought and thought to the spoken word. So the word is the great-grandson of the original source. If the word can produce an effect, judge for yourself how much more powerful would be the preaching through silence.'

This flow of power from the Guru was sometimes transmitted through his eyes. 'Suddenly Bhagavan turned his luminous, transparent eyes on me,' a devotee described the experience. 'Before that I could not stand his gaze for long. Now I looked straight back into those wonderful eyes, how long I could not tell. They held me in a sort of vibration, distinctly audible to me.' Such an experience was always followed by the conviction that the devotee had been taken up by Bhagavan and that henceforth he would be guided.

'It is impossible to be in frequent contact with the Maharshi,' wrote another devotee, 'without becoming lit up inwardly, as it were, mentally illuminated by a sparkling ray from his spiritual orb. Again and again I become conscious that he is drawing my mind into his own atmosphere, during these periods of quiet repose. And it is at such times that one begins to understand why the silences of this man are more significant than his utterances. His quiet, unhurried poise veils a dynamic attainment which can powerfully affect a person without the medium of audible speech or visible action. There are moments when I feel this power of his so greatly, that I know he has only to issue the most disturbing command and I will readily obey it. But the Maharshi is the last person in the world to place his followers in the chains of servile obedience and allows everyone the utmost freedom of action.'

Sri Ramana called silence, 'the true *upadesha* (teaching), the perfect *upadesha*, suited only for the most advanced seeker. The others are unable to draw full inspiration from it. Therefore they require words to explain the truth. But truth is beyond words. It does not admit of explanation. All that it is possible to do is to indicate it. The Guru's silence is the loudest *upadesha*. It is also Grace in its highest form. If the Guru is silent, the seeker's mind gets purified by itself.'

In reply to a question whether the Guru's silence could bring about Self realization, Bhagavan answered, 'In the proximity of the Guru, the *vasanas* (deep-rooted, inherent mental tendencies) cease to be active, the mind becomes still and *samadhi* (the direct experience of the Self) results. Thus the disciple gains true knowledge and right experience in the presence of the Guru. To remain unshaken in it, further efforts are necessary. Eventually the disciple will know it to be his real being and will thus be liberated even while alive.'

One such experience of *samadhi* in the presence of Bhagavan was described by Paul Brunton.

'I enter the hall when the evening meditation period is half over. I slip quietly to the floor and straightaway assume my regular meditation posture. In a few seconds I compose myself and bring all wandering thoughts to a strong centre.

'The Maharshi's seated form floats in a vivid manner before my mind's eye. Following his frequently repeated

instruction, I endeavour to pierce through the mental picture into that which is formless, his real being and inner nature his soul. To my surprise the effort meets with almost instant success and the picture disappear again, leaving me with nothing more than a strongly felt sense of his intimate presence....

'But how to divorce oneself from the age old tyranny of thoughts? I remember that the Maharshi had never suggested that I should attempt to force the stoppage of thinking.

'Trace thought to its place of origin,' is his reiterated counsel. 'Watch for the real self to reveal itself and then your thoughts will die down of their own accord.'

'I surrender myself to complete passivity until I discover the correctness of the sage's prophecy. The waves of thought naturally begin to diminish. The strangest sensation I have experienced till now grips me. Time seems to reel dizzily as the antennae of my rapidly growing intuition begins to reach out into the unknown.....

'Finally it happens. Thought is extinguished like a snuffed candle. I perceive what the Maharshi has confidently affirmed, that the mind takes its rise in a transcendental source. The brain passed into a state of complete suspension, as it does in deep sleep, yet there is not the slightest loss of consciousness. Something that is far superior to the unimportant personality which was I, some deeper, divine being rises into consciousness and becomes me and with it arises an amazing new sense of absolute freedom.. I find myself outside the rim of world consciousness... in the midst of an ocean of blazing light, incredibly alive... my arms embrace all creation with profound sympathy... my heart is remoulded in rapture....'

'You have been in a spiritual trance for nearly two hours,' a devotee informed Brunton when he returned to ordinary consciousness. 'The Maharshi watched you closely all the time. I believe his thoughts guided you.'

CHAPTER NINE

Sri Ramana's care and compassion for all those who approached him, his accessibility, continued right up to the end of his life. In early 1949 a small growth appeared below the elbow of his left arm. It was removed by the doctor of the *ashram*, but returned within a month, larger and more painful. This time it was diagnosed as cancer and there was general alarm. It was operated upon again by doctors from Madras but the malignant tumour reappeared larger than before, higher up on the arm.

Twice more it was surgically removed, but each time it returned. It reached the shoulder, went inwards and poisoned the entire system.

The pain must have been excruciating but Sri Ramana's complete indifference to it amazed his doctors.

On each of their visits he remained more concerned about their welfare than his own worsening condition. His first questions to them invariably were whether they had eaten their food and were being looked after.

Until it became physically impossible for him, Sri Ramana maintained his daily routine. He bathed an hour before sunrise, sat up morning and evening to give *darshan* to his devotees in the new hall built in 1949 to accommodate the ever-growing number of visitors.

After January 1950 he was too unwell and drained of energy to sit in the hall. He shifted to a small room with an adjoining bathroom, east of the hall. His couch was placed in the narrow verandah outside this room, so

that anxious devotees gathering in their hundreds, could still have his *darshan*. Later when he was too weak even for this, devotees filed past the open door of his room, morning and evening.

In the last months, his infectious laugh may have seldom been heard but his sense of humour stayed till the end. 'Why do you worry' he joked with his doctors, when the tumour reappeared, 'It is its nature to come up!' He repeatedly asserted that the death of the body was no reason to grieve. When in spite of that, he heard a devotee knocking her head in grief against a post outside his room, he said, 'O, I thought someone was trying to break a coconut!'

In his serene submission to the long months of pain and suffering he showed that such serenity was possible for those who had anchored in the true Self. Those still struggling to accept the approaching physical separation from him, he reassured saying,' I am not going away. Where could I go? I am here.'

All wondered why so saintly a man should have been subjected to so devastating a disease. Many believed that the sage took upon himself the pains and burdens of those who came to him for help as Lord Shiva had drunk poison to save the world from destruction.

The end of Sri Ramana's earthly existence came on the evening of April 14, 1950. In the days just before, each devotee had received from him a direct, luminous, penetrating look of recognition, experienced as a parting infusion of his Grace. Devotees were singing his beloved composition—Arunachala Shiva, as breath gently left his body. And a shining star trailed slowly across the sky towards the sacred peak of Arunachala.

This holy hill which Bhagavan Sri Ramana Maharishi sought as a child, found and never left again, is permeated now by his invisible presence. Devotees still flock to it, for inspiration and for guidance.

Maurice Frydman, a Polish devotee, voiced the thoughts of many when he wrote, 'The burning regret is that full advantage was not taken of those happy and precious days when Bhagavan was also physically with us—eating, talking, laughing, welcoming all, open to all. The reality was there, but we enclosed ourselves in timidity, in self deception...

'To find him again we must overcome the very obstacles which prevented us from seeing him as he was and going with him where he wanted to take us.

'We ripen when we refuse to drift, when striving ceaselessly becomes the very way of life, when dispassion born of insight becomes spontaneous, when the search 'Who am I' becomes the only thing that matters.

He is there and waiting timelessly. It is we who keep him waiting.'

BIBLIOGRAPHY

Ramana Maharshi by Arthur Osborne,
Jaico Publishing House, Mumbai

Timeless in Time—A Biography by A.R. Natarajan,
Ramana Maharshi Centre for Learning, Bangalore

Be As You Are—The Teachings of Sri Ramana Maharshi
edited by David Godman, Penguin Books India

The Power of the Presence—Transforming Encounters with
Sri Ramana Maharshi Parts I & II
edited by David Godman, Avadhuta Foundation, USA

A Secret India by Paul Brunton,
Srishti Publishers, New Delhi

For more information, contact Ramana Kendra, 8 Institutional Area, Lodi Road, New Delhi-110 003.